THE EL PASO CHILE COMPANY
rum
& tiki
cookbook

THE EL PASO CHILE COMPANY

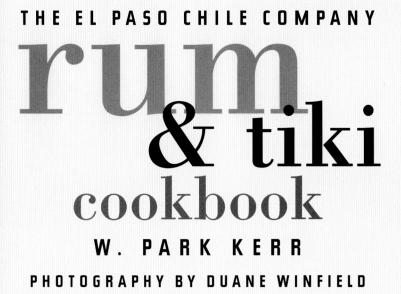

rum & tiki
cookbook

W. PARK KERR

PHOTOGRAPHY BY DUANE WINFIELD

WILLIAM MORROW

AN IMPRINT OF HARPERCOLLINSPUBLISHERS

FIRST EDITION

Designed by Elizabeth Van Itallie
Photography by Duane Winfield
Food styling by Kevin Crafts
Prop styling by Robyn Glaser

Printed on acid-free paper

Library of Congress Cataloging-in-Publication Data has
been applied for.

ISBN 0-688-17760-3

00 01 02 03 04 QKH 10 9 8 7 6 5 4 3 2 1

To Minki La Rue . . . sister, rum runner,
drinking buddy, and pal . . . Love, Park

Boy, what a rummy bunch of the most talented book people on earth. First, my admiration and gratitude to my collaborator-writer, Michael McLaughlin, for his brilliant work, impeccable taste, and insight on this book.

And, once again, the creative dream team: photographer Duane Winfield, food stylist Kevin Crafts, and prop stylist Robyn Glazer. And finally . . . the world's coolest editor, Justin Schwartz, who has one hell of a creative vision and is just plain fun to work with. My sincerest thank you and like they say in the Islands . . . Mai tai, baby! ! !

Park Kerr

contents

introduction

Rum is big. No, rum is huge. Though produced mainly in the Caribbean, it is enjoyed around the world, and every place where rum is drunk, the clouds roll back and the sky and the sea are blue. Rum is tropical island sunshine, bottled.

Rum has history, diversity, and, lately, a rejuvenated popularity. "The new vodka," they're saying, at least in the United States, and the kids who were tippling Chocolate Martinis last week, now have their noses deep in Zombies, Hurricanes, and Mojitos. In less trend-oriented places (anywhere but here), rum has always been king. It is the most popular distilled spirit (Bacardi is the best selling individual liquor brand on the planet). Shockingly, rum even outsells tequila in Mexico, and, also somewhat shocking, was once one of Puritan New England's principal industrial products.

Rum begins with a simple thing—sugar—but is transformed by man and his industrial light and magic into a spirit so varied, so delicious, and so woven into history that it could serve to link more than a few chapters in the story of civilization. Or would, if historians ever took a break for happy hour.

Thirsty yet? Never one to let the homework interfere with the party, let me now go on to say that the good times are never better than when rum is in the glass and on the lip. From the hot and sultry days of summer to the icy heart of winter; from luau to ski lodge; from fruit-bedecked Mai Tai to steaming Hot Buttered Rum to a snifter of oak-aged, vanilla-scented Martinique "rhum" sipped in a big, comfy chair, I celebrate rum in all its sweet, sunny glory.

It's a big subject for a small book, but I've worked to pack in the essentials. Classic rum coolers, frisky New Age rum inventions, and mellow hot rum potions—all are covered here in their infinite variety. Rum as beverage is then joined by rum the cooking ingredient. Few spirits are as agreeable in the kitchen as rum, and at my house (and soon, I hope, at yours), it easily finds its way into everything from bean dip and barbecue sauce to French toast and flan.

So get out the cocktail shaker (in that cupboard—behind the fondue pot), squeeze some limes, and crack open a fresh bottle of Caribbean sunshine. Add some ice and start to work that shaker to a reggae beat, and you're on your way to a great party, mon.

- Sugarcane originated in China and India and was brought to the Caribbean by Columbus on his second voyage.
- Rum was first distilled from sugarcane by Spanish and Portuguese settlers in Brazil.
- Rum was once called "kill-devil," after the belief that the steam escaping from the still had the power to ward off evil.
- Even today, rum plays an essential part in various voodoo rituals.

how rum is made

Rum is distilled from fermented sugar products, chiefly fresh cane juice, cane syrup, or molasses. The process is begun when yeast is added to the sugar product; the resulting mixture is heated and the steam, which condenses as it cools, is raw rum.

The two great styles of rum—light and dark—derive from whether dark molasses or a lighter sugar product is used to start the process. In the Caribbean, rum styles vary from island to island. While most produce various type rums, in general, English-speaking islands are known for molasses-based dark rums, while former French and Spanish colonies excel at lighter, even white, rums.

The type of still also affects the finished rum. Old-fashioned pot stills, frequently heated over an open wood fire, resemble the type of contraption you might associate with "Dogpatch"-style rural American bootleggers. ("Hillbilly," I believe, is no longer politically correct.) These are also called "batch" stills, and produce lower-alcohol, darker rums in small batches. Coffey or continuous column stills are modern improvements to the process, and can run continuously for weeks or months before needing maintenance. Their output is purer, clearer, higher in alcohol, and less distinctively flavored.

The raw rum is variously tinkered with: Additives like sherry may be introduced; very strong rums are diluted with water to a desirable proof; the product may be aged in previously used, charred white oak barrels; and rums from various years may be blended with others to achieve a standardized product.

The finished rums vary widely in color, quality, smoothness, and subtleties of taste, but all retain an underlying sweetness that marks them as deriving from sugarcane.

shopping for rum

Once you discover the wide and wonderful world of rum, it's unlikely that you will limit your basic home bar to just one (however versatile) bottle of white Puerto Rican rum. Even a modest selection would number at least five types, by my count, and a serious aficionado will want to have even more.

Rums are classified on the basis of their raw ingredients (generally molasses vs. something lighter), their proof or alcoholic strength, and their prebottle aging, if any. There are at least 150 rums produced in the Caribbean. Even an above-average liquor store will only begin to scratch the surface, and so I will not go into specific brands. (For the best rum education, schedule an island cruise of a year or two aboard a well-appointed yacht, with someone else doing the driving.) Carefully read the colorful labels on the brands you do find for the essential information you'll need to differentiate them. The general categories are:

WHITE, LIGHT, OR SILVER RUMS Clear and lightly sweet of flavor, these neutral rums are particularly suitable in cocktails.

GOLDEN, ORO, OR AMBRÉ RUMS A brief aging in oak barrels, along with the optional addition of caramel coloring, render these smooth rums golden. They contribute a slightly more robust flavor to cocktails or can be sipped neat.

DARK RUMS Produced in pot stills, sometimes modified by additives and aged in well-charred barrels, these lower-proof rums display a range of bittersweet flavor that molasses lovers (or haters) will instantly recognize. They may be sipped neat, will shine alone in certain drinks, or can bolster the flavor of cocktails made with less aggressive rums.

AGED OR AÑEJO RUMS Or, from French-speaking islands, "*rhums vieux.*" Like good cognac, small batch bourbons, and single malt scotches, these more expensive, frequently blended, barrel-aged rums should be sipped from snifters. The improving all happens in the barrel; once bottled, the essential character of the rum does not change.

SINGLE MARK RUMS These rare rums are not blended, but come from a single batch or cask. Unpredictable, variable, and very expensive, these are for the collecting connoisseur.

FLAVORED OR SPICED RUMS For the younger set. Popular additions are spices, vanilla, various fruit, assorted citrus, and coconut. All contribute extra flavor to certain festive cocktails.

OVERPROOF RUMS Extremely potent, also flammable, these rums are epitomized by Bacardi's 151-proof rum. Breathtakingly rough to drink straight, but often used in small amounts to boost the alcohol content of a number of classic cocktails.

classic

coolers

my daiquiri

This best known of rum drinks is generally attributed to one Jennings Cox, a mining engineer stationed in Santiago, Cuba, in the sizzling summer of 1898. While he may have originally concocted it to fight off malarial infection (the rum) and scurvy (the lime), a properly made Daiquiri these days is not, in the strict sense, medicinal. My semiclassic version is potent and more than a little reminiscent of my *other* favorite cocktail, the Margarita. To transform this into another classic cocktail, the Bacardi, add 1 teaspoon grenadine.

> A wedge of lime
> Granulated sugar on a small plate
> 3 ounces gold rum
> 1½ ounces fresh lime juice
> 1½ teaspoons superfine sugar
> 1 teaspoon curaçao or other orange liqueur

Run the lime wedge around the rim of a stemmed cocktail glass. Dip the moistened rim in the sugar on the plate. Set the lime wedge and the glass aside.

In a cocktail shaker, combine the rum, lime juice, superfine sugar, and curaçao. Stir with a long spoon to dissolve the sugar. Add ice cubes to fill the shaker about half full and shake well.

Half-fill the prepared glass with crushed ice if desired. Strain the Daiquiri into the glass, squeeze the lime wedge into the cocktail, discard, and serve immediately.

RUM 101 As rum comes from sugar, so it goes to sugar. You may not normally sweeten your cocktails, but I think you'll find that, when it comes to rum, a little sugar, especially when lime juice is present, nicely balances the flavor.

planter's punch

It's easy to get into a Caribbean state of mind with one of these tall coolers in your fist. A hammock on a wide veranda, above a field of sugarcane stirring in the trade winds, with the blue sea distantly visible—these are the images rum stirs up when I stir up a Planter's Punch. Santa Fe chef Mark Miller is my source for the use of vanilla in this cocktail, a touch of tropical genius you have got to try.

2 ounces gold rum
1½ ounces fresh orange juice
1½ ounces unsweetened pineapple juice
1 ounce dark rum
1 tablespoon curaçao or other orange liqueur
1 tablespoon fresh lime juice
1 teaspoon grenadine
½ teaspoon Vanilla Rum (page 105) or vanilla extract
2 or 3 dashes Angostura bitters
A slice of orange and a maraschino cherry on a cocktail pick,
   as garnish

In a tall glass, combine all the ingredients except the fruit garnish. Stir to blend, then fill the glass with ice cubes. Add the garnish and serve immediately.

RUM 101 The standard double-sided cocktail measuring device—the jigger—has a 1-ounce measure on one side and a 1½-ounce measure on the other, thus providing all the possible combinations one needs to build a great rum cocktail. If you're jiggerless, just remember that 1 ounce equals 2 tablespoons—get out the measuring spoons and multiply or divide accordingly.

mai

MAKES 1 COCKTAIL

The Mai Tai is a great drink, much debased. Order one in most bars and you'll be served something akin to Hawaiian Punch and kerosene, festively garnished with a plastic cocktail parasol. Trader Vic Bergeron's almond-scented original, on the other hand, was so good the first people to taste it, Tahitian friends of his, are said to have named it by exclaiming, *"Mai tai—roa ae!"* which translates to "Out of this world—the best!" Here is how to achieve that otherworldly perfection, adapted only slightly from Vic's original.

> 2½ ounces gold rum (Vic preferred 17-year-old J. Wray and Nephew brand)
>
> 1 ounce fresh lime juice
>
> 1 tablespoon dark rum
>
> 1 tablespoon curaçao or other orange liqueur
>
> 2 teaspoons orgeat (almond syrup, available in some liquor stores)
>
> 1 teaspoon grenadine
>
> A spear of pineapple and a maraschino cherry on a cocktail pick and a plastic parasol, as garnish

In a cocktail shaker half-filled with ice cubes, combine the gold rum, lime juice, dark rum, curaçao, orgeat, and grenadine. Shake until very cold. Pour into a stemmed cocktail glass along with any remaining ice or strain into a tall glass and add fresh ice. Garnish and serve immediately.

RUM 101 Curaçao, made from the peels of fragrant bitter oranges grown on the Caribbean island of the same name, often finds its way into my rum cocktails. Unless I specify blue curaçao, use only the clear or "white" version. Triple sec or Cointreau can be substituted or, for the silver spoon set, Grand Marnier.

piña

Created in one Puerto Rican hotel or other, in the late fifties or early sixties (accounts vary), this drink's name translates as "strained pineapple," ironic since it is the sweet and viscous coconut "cream" that has become its main ingredient. (To steal a line from comedian Bobcat Goldthwait, this product appears to "have as many artificial ingredients as a car battery.") Here is my lighter Piña Colada for the new millennium, made with coconut milk—the kind used in Thai cooking—rather than coconut cream, and including plenty of fresh pineapple.

⅓ cup finely chopped fresh pineapple
2½ ounces coconut-flavored rum
¼ cup Thai-style coconut milk
1 tablespoon fresh lime juice
1 tablespoon sugar
A thin wedge of pineapple and a slice of lime, as garnish

In a blender, combine all the ingredients except the garnish. Blend briefly to partially puree the pineapple. Add six ice cubes from a home-style freezer tray and blend on high until smooth and frothy. Pour into any tall fancy glass of your choice, garnish, and serve immediately.

colada

charles h. baker jr.'s
"improved"

Baker, author of the two-volume *The Gentleman's Companion*, published in 1946, was a contemporary of Hemingway and Trader Vic. He spent much of his time as they appear to have, sunburnt, a little buzzed on good rum, yarning and yachting his way from island bar to island bar, in pursuit of the good life. Concerned that his drinks be strong but not too sweet, Baker simply but brilliantly remodeled this Cuban classic: Mashing the limes to release their oils adds a welcome bitter edge and deserves Baker's favorite toast: "*Salud y pesetas!*"

¼ large lime, in 2 pieces
One 8-ounce bottle chilled Coca-Cola
2 ounces white or gold rum

In a tall glass, with the back of the bowl of a long spoon, mash the lime pieces, extracting all their juice and fragrant oil. Add the rum and stir. Fill the glass three-quarters full with ice cubes. Add Coke until the drink is the strength you desire (Baker-style, you may not use it all). Stir to blend and serve immediately.

cuba libre

This legendarily strong drink—sometimes called the Brazilian Daiquiri—is traditionally made with *cachaça*, a rough sugarcane liquor that is not readily located in the United States. Rum is a close enough cousin, however, to stand in for it with excellent results. The cocktail gets its intense lime fragrance from crushing the fruit to release the oils from the peels. Make a big pitcher and serve this at your next backyard barbecue (preferably a Brazilian-style one featuring grilled steaks) or just mix up a single from this formula. It goes against the fiery nature of the Caipirinha, but a splash of soda can be added to civilize things slightly.

1 large lime, cut into 8 pieces
2 tablespoons turbinado or Demerara sugar
1 ounce white rum
1 ounce 151-proof rum

In a tall glass, using the handle end of a large wooden spoon, thoroughly crush the lime pieces together with the sugar to release their juices and oil. Add the two rums and stir well. (If the sugar hasn't all dissolved, let things sit for a few minutes and then stir some more.) Add three ice cubes from a home-style freezer tray and stir one last time. Enjoy—slowly.

RUM 101 Granular turbinado sugar retains much of the cane's original molasses and thus has a richer flavor than that of more highly refined white sugar. Demerara sugar is a particular turbinado sugar that comes from Guyana, also the home of much of the molasses used in rum manufacture in the Caribbean. Turbinado sugar is readily found in supermarkets in this country under the Sugar in the Raw label, or in health food stores.

mojito

Often called "the national drink of Cuba," the Mojito is unknown to most Americans and will be a wonderful surprise when finally sampled: Few rum drinks are so pretty, tasty, and refreshing. The reestablishment of diplomatic relations with Cuba remains doubtful, but if this libation is any indication of the possibilities, America will surely benefit from the change.

    4 sprigs fresh mint
    1½ tablespoons superfine sugar
    1½ ounces white or gold rum
    1½ tablespoons fresh lime juice
    2 to 3 dashes Angostura bitters
    Club soda

In a tall glass with the back of the bowl of a long spoon, gently mash together three sprigs of the mint and the sugar (bruise the mint leaves without actually breaking them up). Add the rum, lime juice, and bitters and stir to dissolve the sugar. Fill the glass about three-quarters full of ice. Add club soda until the drink is the strength you desire (don't drown it) Stir with the spoon to blend, garnish with the remaining sprig of mint, and serve immediately.

RUM 101 Angostura bitters, developed in the nineteenth century by a German doctor who served in Simón Bolívar's army of liberation, is a potent blend of alcohol, herbs, and other aromatics. Taken in soda it will settle the stomach, it makes Pink Gin pink and turns up in more than a few rum cocktails, for which it has a unique affinity. Originally produced in Angostura, Venezuela, it is now manufactured on the island of Trinidad, at a distillery that also produces rum from South American molasses. It contains quite a lot of alcohol (presumably rum, although that's not clear) and has the vanillalike power to make cocktails—also foods and even desserts—taste better without actually tasting like bitters.

pink

Last in alphabetically organized bar guides, but first in the hearts and minds of Spring Breakers everywhere, the Zombie—if prepared with some attention to proportion, and with top-notch ingredients—has much to recommend it. With its velvety power disguised by plenty of bright fruit flavor, it's no drink for amateurs, but it will certainly liven up a party. Why a *Pink* Zombie? Even scarier than the regular kind, I figure. You may skip the Hawaii Five-O–type garnishes on every other drink in this book if you must, but a Zombie, especially a pink one, calls for all the adornment you can provide.

1½ ounces white or gold rum

1 ounce passion fruit syrup (available in gourmet shops and some liquor stores)

1 ounce unsweetened pineapple juice

1 ounce pink grapefruit juice

1½ tablespoons dark rum

4 teaspoons fresh lime juice

1 tablespoon crème de banane or apricot brandy

2 teaspoons grenadine

2 teaspoons 151-proof rum

Many festive garnishes, including a spear of pineapple, a slice of orange, and a maraschino cherry on a cocktail pick, a lime round, plus plastic monkeys, parasols, etc.

In a blender, combine all the ingredients except the 151-proof rum and the garnishes. Add five ice cubes from a home-style freezer tray. Blend until foamy. Transfer to a tall, exotic glass. Float the 151-proof rum atop the drink by slowly drizzling it onto the bowl of a spoon inverted over the cocktail. Garnish and serve immediately.

jack's
curaçao
cooler

This version of a very tasty and refreshing classic comes from author Jack Gantos, who grew up in the Caribbean and, when it comes to rum, knows whereof he speaks. Keep in mind that dark rum is lower in proof than light, so while this drink's flavor is robust, its octane is modest.

⅓ cup fresh orange juice
2 ounces dark rum
1 tablespoon curaçao or other orange liqueur
1 tablespoon fresh lime juice
Club soda (optional)
A wedge of lime

In a tall glass, combine the orange juice, rum, curaçao, and lime juice. Stir to blend. Fill the glass about three-quarters full of ice and stir again. Add a splash of soda (don't drown it), if desired, squeeze the lime wedge into the glass, discard, and serve immediately.

MAKES 1 COCKTAIL

This is my version of O'Brien's Hurricane, a classic cocktail every tourist to New Orleans samples. Its specially designed glass has been named after it, with the cost of the glass worked into the price of the drink, to cover its assumed theft by pre-forgiven souvenir hunters. At home, theft will probably not be an issue, but a round or two of Hurricanes always stirs up New Orleans–style good times. Look for passion fruit juice at gourmet shops and health food stores.

1½ ounces white rum
1 ounce dark rum
1 ounce passion fruit juice or nectar
1 ounce fresh lime juice
2 teaspoons superfine sugar
A wedge of lime

In a cocktail shaker, combine the white and dark rums, passion fruit juice, lime juice, and sugar. Half-fill with ice cubes and shake until very cold. Strain over fresh ice in a hurricane glass or pour into a stemmed glass with the ice chips that remain in the shaker. Squeeze the lime wedge into the drink, discard, and serve immediately.

hurricane

rum milk

MAKES 1 COCKTAIL

Not all rum coolers are tall and tropical. This soothing classic, suitable for easing you into the morning after and mellow enough for a festive brunch, particularly one on Christmas or New Year's Day, is one of my favorites. If you're entertaining a crowd, stir up a pitcherful (without ice) and let it chill overnight, then ladle it over ice in punch cups or something similar the next day.

⅓ cup milk
1 ounce gold rum
1 ounce Tia Maria
¼ teaspoon Vanilla Rum (page 105) or vanilla extract
Pinch of freshly grated nutmeg

In a shaker half-filled with ice, combine all the ingredients. Shake until very cold. Pour into an old-fashioned glass or strain into a stemmed cocktail glass and serve immediately.

RUM 101 Tia Maria is a coffee liqueur, a little lighter and less sweet than Kahlúa. It is produced in Jamaica from Blue Mountain coffee beans and has a great natural affinity for rum.

It takes only minutes to make your own eggnog from scratch. On top of that, homemade tastes infinitely better than the nasty stuff that comes in cartons, and since it needs to chill thoroughly anyway (eggnog is not traditionally served over ice), the work is conveniently done well before the guests come caroling at your door. This is a rum book, so it's an all-rum nog, but you can replace up to half the rum with bourbon or brandy, if desired.

12 large eggs
1 cup superfine sugar
2 quarts half-and-half
3 cups gold rum
1 cup dark rum
4 teaspoons Vanilla Rum (page 105) or vanilla extract
½ teaspoon salt
Freshly grated nutmeg, for serving

In a large mixing bowl, using a handheld electric mixer, if desired, beat the eggs until light. Beat in the sugar. Mix in the half-and-half, gold and dark rums, vanilla, and salt. Cover and chill well, at least 5 hours and preferably overnight.

Strain the eggnog into a punch bowl. Set out a shaker of freshly grated nutmeg and let each guest sprinkle on his or her own.

eggnog

rum

adventures

lemon rum
martini

Don't fiddle with a classic, unless you can at least come close to matching the original, is my motto. The icy elegance of the Martini especially defies improvement, but here is one reworking that works. Bacardi Limon is a fairly new entry in that company's product line, and the fresh lemony-flavored result makes a great Martini. I keep the rum in the freezer and the vermouth in the fridge, for a breathlessly cold cocktail.

2 ounces very cold lemon-flavored rum
1 teaspoon chilled dry white vermouth
4 pitted black olives, preferably Kalamatas, on a cocktail pick, as garnish

Fill a cocktail shaker half-full with ice. Add the rum and vermouth and shake until very, very cold. Strain into a stemmed cocktail glass or strain into a rocks glass over fresh ice. Garnish with the olive pick and serve immediately.

RUM 101 All ice used in cocktail making should be dry—not "dry ice," but ice free from surface water, which dilutes the drink. The best ice is cracked from a home-style tray from a very cold freezer just seconds before the cocktail is assembled. If you've done things right, the rum will "smoke" as it hits the ice and you'll have a great (nonwatery) drink.

blackberry-

Batidos are Latino fruit shakes, lighter than milk shakes or even smoothies, and thus very suitable for the various hot-weather countries where they are enjoyed. Transforming the general idea of the refreshing Batido into a refreshing but potent cocktail took me no time at all—the hard part was choosing which fruit to use. I settled on blackberries, but the sky's really the limit: Use whatever is ripe, colorful, and intensely flavored.

1 cup fresh blackberries, picked over
2 ounces white or gold rum
¼ cup sweetened condensed milk
1 tablespoon fresh lime juice

In a blender, combine all the ingredients. Add five ice cubes from a standard home-style freezer tray. Blend on high speed until smooth and frothy. Transfer to a tall, exotic glass and serve immediately.

batido

coconut
breeze

MAKES 1 COCKTAIL

In my opinion, the invention of coconut-flavored rum was a great milestone of progress, rum-wise. Its light but distinct flavor boost improves any number of simple but refreshing drinks without adding extra-fuss time for the bartender. Rum and pineapple juice is a drink as old as, well, rum and pineapple juice, but add the scent and taste of coconut and you've got a drink that just cries out for sand, surf, and "one more, please."

⅓ cup unsweetened pineapple juice (see Rum 101 below)
2 ounces coconut-flavored rum
1 tablespoon fresh lime juice
1½ teaspoons superfine sugar
Club soda
A wedge of lime

In a tall glass, combine the pineapple juice, rum, lime juice, and sugar. Stir to dissolve the sugar. Fill the glass three-quarters full with ice and stir to blend. Top with a splash of soda (don't drown it), squeeze the lime wedge into the drink, discard, and serve immediately.

RUM 101 For a change of pace, replace half the pineapple juice with mango or guava nectar.

melon-tamarind liquado

Like Batidos, Mexican Liquados are light, fruit-based drinks, made with a bit of milk but not normally including alcohol. Rum has such an affinity for nearly all fruits, however; my notion of adding a splash of the golden stuff to a Cantaloupe Liquado is hardly revolutionary. Tart tamarind "water," the thinned and sieved paste derived from the pods of a tropical tree, adds welcome complexity to the flavor of the drink.

1 cup diced very ripe cantaloupe (about one fourth a
    medium melon)
2 ounces gold rum
3 tablespoons milk
2 tablespoons honey
1 ounce tamarind water (see Rum 101 below)
1 tablespoon fresh lime juice

In a blender, combine all the ingredients. Add five ice cubes from a home-style freezer tray and blend on high speed until smooth and frothy. Transfer to two tall, exotic glasses and serve immediately.

RUM 101 The most common form in which tamarind is found in this country in Latin markets is in something called "seedless" paste. It is brown, sticky, and packed with seeds and fibers that need to be removed. Pull off a 2-ounce blob of the paste. In a blender, combine it with ¾ cup very hot tap water and let stand 10 minutes, pulsing briefly once or twice (avoid breaking up the seeds). Then pulse several more times. Transfer to a sieve set over a bowl and press as much of the softened paste and its liquid through the sieve as you can. Scrape the excess off the bottom of the sieve and stir it into the liquid in the bowl. Discard the seeds. Unused tamarind water can be frozen.

three-red-fruit cooler

Pomegranates begin to come into season at about the same time watermelons reach their peak, which put the idea for this light and very refreshing cocktail into my head. (As for the cranberry juice, well, I had some open.) Getting the juice out of a pomegranate can be a challenge, but the alternative, grenadine, in effect an artificial pomegranate syrup, is not suitable here.

1½ cups cubed (½-inch) seedless red ripe watermelon
Juice from 1 large pomegranate, about ¼ cup
2 ounces white rum
1 ounce cranberry juice cocktail
1 ounce fresh lime juice
1 tablespoon curaçoa or other orange liqueur
1 tablespoon superfine sugar
2 wedges of lime

Combine all the ingredients in a blender. Add five ice cubes from a home-style freezer tray and blend on high speed until smooth and frothy. Transfer to two tall exotic glasses, squeeze a lime wedge into each drink, discard, and serve immediately.

RUM 101 To juice a pomegranate, roll it around on a flat work surface, pressing gently with the palm of your hand, until it is fairly soft. Holding the pomegranate over a sieve set over a bowl, gently cut it open. Inside will be juice, white pulp, and many seeds, each enclosed in a small sac of crimson liquid. Scoop the seeds into the sieve and discard the peel and pulp. Gently press and squeeze the seeds to pop the juice sacs. Avoid too much pressure, which can make the juice bitter. Be persistent. A good-sized pomegranate should yield at least ¼ cup juice.

Technically, this is not a Rickey, but I loved the name, so what the hell. Tall, crisp, light, and gingery, and fragrant with fresh lemongrass, this is one of the greatest antidotes to hot weather and hot food you'll ever stir up. Look for a premium, extra-spicy ginger ale. I get a good one at the health food store.

One 6-inch stalk very fresh lemongrass
2 ounces white or gold rum
1 teaspoon fresh lime juice
Ginger ale
A wedge of lime

Cut the lemongrass crosswise into 1-inch pieces. In the bottom of a tall glass, using the handle end of a wooden spoon or something similar, crush the lemongrass to release its flavor and scent. Add the rum and lime juice. Fill the glass three-quarters full with ice. Add ginger ale to taste (don't drown the drink). Stir briefly to blend, squeeze the lime wedge into the drink, discard, and serve immediately.

rickey

frozen
mango-peach

I remember a rather eccentric friend of mine who, when asked by her large brood of children what she wanted for her fortieth birthday menu, chose frozen fruit Daiquiris and escargots. Nothing is more festive than a frozen Daiquiri, unless it's a canned snail: Still, it was a great party. Combining two compatible fruits leads to a whole much greater than the sum of the parts. Don't scoff: These are really worth drinking.

½ cup chopped very ripe peach, plus 2 thin wedges
  for garnish
½ cup chopped ripe mango, plus 2 thin wedges for garnish
4 ounces white or gold rum
3 tablespoons fresh lime juice
2 tablespoons superfine sugar
2 wedges of lime

In a blender combine all the ingredients and blend until fairly smooth. Add six ice cubes from a home-style freezer tray and blend on high speed until smooth and frothy. Divide between two tall, exotic glasses, garnish with the fruit, squeeze a lime wedge into each glass, discard, and serve immediately.

RUM 101 Superfine sugar is exactly what it sounds like—sugar more finely granulated than the regular kind, ideal for dissolving in cold liquids, like cocktails, without leaving a sweet slurry in the bottom of the glass. It's found in the sugar section of some supermarkets, and occasionally in liquor stores, labeled "bar sugar." In a pinch, confectioners' sugar can be substituted.

two worlds
cooler

Italian Galliano joins Caribbean rum in this drink whose subtle, sweet, and herbaceous flavor might well unite the hemispheres. Tastes good, too.

1½ ounces gold rum
1½ tablespoons Galliano
⅓ cup unsweetened pineapple juice
1 teaspoon fresh lime juice
2 to 3 dashes Angostura bitters
Club soda

In a tall glass, combine the rum, Galliano, pineapple juice, lime juice, and bitters. Fill the glass three-quarters full with ice. Add a splash of soda (don't drown the drink) and serve immediately.

In 1919, on an unseasonably warm January day in Boston, a steel tank holding over two million gallons of molasses collapsed. The resulting 30-foot-high wave of sticky goo devastated the North End, toppling elevated train tracks, knocking buildings from their foundations, and killing twenty-one people. The sound of gunfire could be heard as injured horses were put out of their misery. Fireboats were used to blast the stuff away with salt water, and for years afterward Boston Harbor was stained brown. Prohibition was on its way and the molasses stockpile was said to have been in anticipation of the outlawing of rum's essential ingredient.

This is my version of a drink created at New York City's The Cocktail Room. I haven't sampled it there and only based this formula on a general description of the original, so any failures of duplication here are mine. For my money, this Day-Glo concoction looks and tastes exactly the way a tropical rum drink should look and taste.

2 ounces white or gold rum
1 ounce crème de banane
1 tablespoon fresh lime juice
2 teaspoons grenadine
A wedge of lime
Assorted fruit, including banana, as garnish

In a shaker, combine the rum, crème de banane, lime juice, and grenadine. Half-fill with ice and shake until very cold. Pour the drink into a stemmed cocktail glass. Squeeze the lime wedge into the glass and discard, garnish with the fruit, and serve immediately.

banana monkey

ice•cream•
daiquiri

Totally indulgent and ideal for those who prefer their drinks to taste a bit like dessert, this one was designed to use Häagen-Dazs pineapple-coconut ice cream, one of several new flavors the ice cream maker has targeted to America's growing Latin market. You can use plain vanilla ice cream, substitute coconut rum, and add a bit of crushed pineapple if the new flavor isn't yet stocked in your neighborhood.

3 medium scoops pineapple-coconut ice cream, softened
2 ounces white or gold rum
¼ cup cold milk

In a blender, combine the ice cream, rum, and milk. Blend on a low speed until almost smooth (a few lumps of ice cream are pleasant). Pour into a tall glass, preferably a soda fountain–type milk shake glass, and serve immediately.

For years, sailors in the British navy were issued a daily ration of rum. When accidents on shipboard became overwhelming, a certain Vice Admiral Vernon suggested diluting the ration with water. He may also have suggested the addition of sugar and lime juice. He was nicknamed "Old Groggram," after the type of fabric he used to trim his cloak, and in time sailors came to call the daily ration "grog," thus honoring the admiral for something other than his military prowess. The daily ration lasted until July 31, 1970.

mauna
kea
cocktail

Here is a devastatingly good after-dinner drink I put together to take advantage of a bottle of macadamia liqueur someone brought me as a present from the islands. I named it for the Hawaiian volcano that despite its tropical location is occasionally snow-capped, here represented by the float of cream atop the drink.

- 1½ ounces best-quality gold rum
- 1 ounce macadamia liqueur
- 1 tablespoon premium chocolate liqueur, such as Godiva
- 1½ tablespoons whipping cream

In a short rocks glass three-quarters filled with ice, combine the rum and the two liqueurs. Stir to blend. Float the whipping cream on top of the drink and serve immediately.

tall
tahitian

One ingredient that shows up a lot in old cocktail books is maraschino, an Italian cherry-based liqueur. Not sweet (not even red), it has a bitter almondish quality that nicely balances some of the sweeter ingredients rum embraces. A bottle will last a long time, and its contributions to your drink making will be considerable.

⅓ cup unsweetened pineapple juice
2 ounces white, gold, or coconut-flavored rum
1½ teaspoons superfine sugar
1½ teaspoons curaçao or other orange liqueur
1½ teaspoons maraschino
Club soda
A wedge of lime
Maraschino cherry, as garnish

In a tall glass, combine the juice, rum, sugar, curaçao, and maraschino. Stir to dissolve the sugar. Fill the glass about three-quarters full with ice and stir to chill. Add a splash of soda (don't drown the drink), squeeze the lime into the glass and discard, garnish with the cherry, and serve immediately.

blue
lagoon

MAKES 1 COCKTAIL

I yield to no man in my admiration for Brooke Shields, hence this elegant aqua concoction. It's a silky sipper that goes down easily—beware.

¼ cup passion fruit juice or nectar
1½ ounces white, gold, or coconut-flavored rum
1 ounce Thai-style coconut milk
1 ounce blue curaçao
1 tablespoon fresh lime juice
2 teaspoons superfine sugar
A wedge of lime
An orchid, as garnish

In a shaker half-filled with ice, combine the passion fruit juice, rum, coconut milk, curaçao, lime juice, and sugar. Shake until very cold. Pour the drink into an exotic glass (or strain it onto fresh ice if desired), squeeze the lime into the glass and discard, garnish with the orchid, and serve immediately.

My Spiced Rum

hot

stuff

When the tip of your nose turns icy and the cold creeps into your bones, the only thing other than a week in Antigua that will warm you up is a properly made Hot Buttered Rum. Using spiced rum (preferably homemade) makes for a particularly stimulating drink, a very romantic concept that caused me to write the recipe to serve two.

> **4 ounces My Spiced Rum (recipe follows) or commercially prepared spiced rum**
> **2 pats (1 ounce total) unsalted butter**
> **14 ounces water**
> **⅓ cup packed dark brown sugar**

Divide the rum between two 12-ounce heatproof mugs. Float a pat of butter in each mug.

In a small, heavy saucepan, stir together the water and sugar. Set over medium heat and bring to a full rolling boil. Ladle the boiling water into the prepared mugs, dividing it evenly, and serve immediately.

hot
buttered
rum

my
spiced
rum

MAKES ¾ LITER

Three hundred years ago, Captain Henry Morgan, a buccaneer-turned-island-governor, began to add spice and fruit flavors to the rum he produced on Jamaica. Today, along with other flavored rums, spiced rums are among the most popular in the world, especially with younger drinkers, a category into which I no longer fit. Still, I love spiced rum and, never one to let well enough alone, am just as happy mixing up my own as I am buying someone else's. A bottle of this spicy, fragrant stuff makes a wonderful Christmas gift.

One 750-milliliter bottle gold rum
Peel from 1 medium orange, removed in a long, thin strip
1 vanilla bean, split lengthwise
One 4-inch cinnamon stick
1 tablespoon whole allspice
4 whole cloves

Pour off about ¼ cup of the rum and reserve it for another use. (You'll find one.) Add the orange peel, vanilla bean, cinnamon stick, allspice, and cloves to the bottle. Cover and let stand for about 2 weeks. The rum is ready when the allspice berries sink to the bottom of the bottle.

See photograph on page 60.

honey
rum
toddy

This is the kind of soothing hot drink that is often prescribed for a sore throat. Don't wait until your next case of the flu to sample it, however: Whenever the weather turns cold, this will cure what ails you.

½ cup boiling water
2 ounces white or gold rum
2 tablespoons honey
1 tablespoon fresh lime juice
A thin slice of lime

Bring a pan of water to a boil. In a 12-ounce heatproof mug, combine the rum, honey, lime juice, and lime slice. Add the boiling water to the mug. Stir well to dissolve the honey and blend the ingredients. Serve immediately.

Flaming after-dinner drinks have a retro appeal I love. Since Jamaica is firmly tied to coffee, through both its Jamaican Blue Mountain coffee and Tia Maria, the coffee liqueur made from those rare and pricey beans, this drink seemed a natural. Thin, fancy glassware may not stand up to the heat: Look for something sturdier at a restaurant supply house.

A wedge of lime
Granulated sugar on a small plate
1 tablespoon 151-proof rum
1½ ounces Tia Maria
1 ounce dark rum, preferably Jamaican
½ cup freshly brewed strong, dark roast coffee
1 tablespoon superfine sugar
Whipped cream, for serving
Chocolate-coated coffee beans, as garnish (optional)

Run the lime around the rim of a 12-ounce heatproof glass or glass mug and discard. Dip the moist rim in the sugar on the plate to coat.

Measure the 151-proof rum into the prepared glass. Tilt the glass and ignite the rum. Working carefully (the flame will be nearly invisible), tilt the glass in all directions to melt the sugar.

Set the glass on a flat surface and add the Tia Maria, dark rum, and coffee; this will extinguish the flames. Add the superfine sugar and stir to dissolve. Top with a dollop of whipped cream, garnish with coffee beans, if desired, and serve. (Use straws to sip this drink at first until the molten sugar cools on the rim of the glass.)

jamaican

A Tom and Jerry is, in effect, a hot eggnog. If you make up the base (or "batter") in advance, you can have one of these body warmers ready to sip mere minutes after the chilled guest arrives. When the holiday season approaches, multiply this formula upward accordingly, borrow an extra blender, and throw a Tom and Jerry party.

2 large eggs
¼ cup confectioners' sugar
2 ounces white or gold rum
1 ounce dark rum
1 ounce brandy
1 cup boiling water
Freshly grated nutmeg

In a bowl, whisk the eggs until foamy. Whisk in the confectioners' sugar. Stir in the rums and the brandy. This batter can be refrigerated for up to 3 days.

For serving, transfer the batter to a blender. Through the hole in the blender cover, with the motor running on a medium speed, gradually add the cup of hot water. Continue to blend until fluffy and slightly thickened, another 10 seconds or so. Divide between two mugs, dust with nutmeg, and serve immediately.

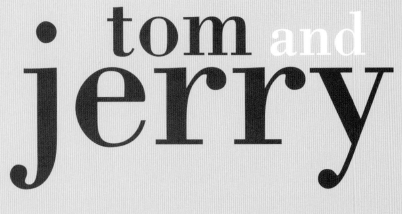

tom and jerry

hot
apple pie

Here rum is combined with another sure-fire heater-upper, the French apple brandy called Calvados. When the rum is spiced rum (ideally homemade) and the Calvados is joined by hot apple cider, the effect is very apple-pie-like. These taste like Christmas to me, although I usually start serving them around about Halloween.

1 ounce My Spiced Rum (page 63) or commercially
   prepared spiced rum
1 ounce Calvados
2 teaspoons superfine sugar
One 4-inch cinnamon stick
½ cup apple cider, preferably filtered
A thin slice of raw apple, as garnish

In a 12-ounce heatproof mug, combine the rum, Calvados, sugar, and cinnamon stick. Bring the cider to a boil. (For such a small amount of liquid, the microwave oven is ideal.) Add the cider to the mug and stir to dissolve the sugar. Garnish with the apple slice and serve immediately.

RUM 101
For an extra-rich Hot Apple Pie, let a pat of butter melt atop the drink.

rum that

really
cooks

plantain chips with rummy • black bean dip

MAKES 8 SERVINGS

For a Tex-Mexican like me, this Caribbean-inspired bean dip is a real change of pace. The unique taste comes from plenty of rum plus achiote (a seasoning paste of annatto seeds and other flavorings found in Latin supermarkets and some gourmet shops) and the scooping tool is not tortilla chips but tostones—twice-fried chips of the starchy root known as the plantain. Not my mama's bean dip, by a long shot, but *muy delicioso*!

2 slices of thickly cut bacon, chopped

1 tablespoon olive oil

½ cup finely chopped yellow onion

½ cup chopped green bell pepper

2 cloves garlic, minced

1 teaspoon ground cumin

1 teaspoon achiote paste

Two 16-ounce cans refried black beans

1 cup canned black beans, well rinsed and drained

½ cup dark rum

1 teaspoon salt

About ⅔ cup sour cream, whisked until smooth

2 scallions, thinly sliced

Tostones (recipe follows)

In a heavy, medium saucepan over low heat, combine the bacon and oil. Cook, stirring occasionally, until the bacon becomes crisp, 8 to 10 minutes. Add the yellow onion, green pepper, garlic, cumin, and achiote and cook, stirring often, until the vegetables become tender, about 10 minutes. Stir in the refried beans, black beans, rum, and the salt. Bring to a simmer and cook partially covered, stirring often, until the mixture is thick and the flavor of raw alcohol has dissipated, about 25 minutes. Adjust the seasoning.

Spoon the dip into a serving bowl. Drizzle it with the sour cream and scatter the scallions over all. Serve immediately, accompanied with the Tostones for dipping.

tostones

MAKES 8 SERVINGS

Bright green underripe plantains will be starchier and harder to peel; darker specimens will be slightly sweeter and the peels will come off more easily. Both sorts make good Tostones.

4 medium-large plantains, about 2½ pounds total
About 3 cups corn or peanut oil
Salt

Trim off the ends of the plantains. Angle-cut the plantains crosswise in half. Peel the plantains, then angle-cut them into ¼-inch slices.

Add enough oil to a large skillet to make a ¾-inch layer. Over medium heat warm the oil to 325°F. Working in batches if necessary (don't crowd the skillet), cook the plantain slices until they are somewhat tender but not brown, about 3 minutes. With a slotted spoon, transfer the slices to paper towels to drain. Using a tostone press (available in some gourmet shops and in Latin supermarkets), a tortilla press, or a meat pounder, flatten the still-warm plantain rounds. (The thinner the round, the crisper the finished tostone.) The plantain rounds can be prepared to this point several hours in advance.

Set the skillet over medium-high heat and rewarm the oil to 375°F. Working in batches if necessary (don't crowd the skillet), fry the rounds a second time until they are crisp and lightly browned, 4 to 5 minutes. Transfer them to paper towels to drain. Sprinkle with salt to taste. Serve hot or warm.

avocado-rum bisque
with cayenne whipped cream and pistachios

MAKES 6 SERVINGS

Cool and nutty, this celadon soup is a great way to begin a grill meal on a hot summer's night. Rum adds a mysterious sweetness that brings out new depths in the flavor of the avocados, while the nuts add crunch. Macadamias can replace the pistachios.

2 tablespoons unsalted butter

1½ cups chopped yellow onions

1 cup chopped carrots

¼ cup chopped celery

2 cloves garlic, chopped

3½ cups reduced-sodium canned chicken broth

½ cup gold rum

1 teaspoon salt

2 medium-large, ripe California avocados

½ teaspoon hot pepper sauce, such as Tabasco

½ cup heavy cream, whipped to stiff peaks

Cayenne pepper in a shaker jar

⅓ cup coarsely chopped shelled pistachios

In a medium soup pan over moderate heat, melt the butter. Add the onions, carrots, celery, and garlic, cover and cook, stirring once or twice, for 10 minutes. Add the broth, rum, and the salt and bring to a simmer. Partially cover and cook, stirring once or twice, until the vegetables are tender, about 30 minutes. Cool to room temperature.

Halve and pit the avocados and scoop the flesh from the peels. In a food processor, in batches, puree together the soup base and the avocados until smooth. Transfer to a bowl, stir in the pepper sauce, and cover tightly. Chill until cold, no more than 3 hours.

Adjust the seasoning. Divide the soup among six chilled bowls. Top each with a dollop of the whipped cream. Dust the whipped cream generously to taste with cayenne. Sprinkle the pistachios over and around the cream. Serve immediately.

grilled shrimp
coconut-rum
with . . .

MAKES 4 TO 6 SERVINGS

Coconut shrimp and peanut sauce are two phrases dear to my heart. Here they are paired up in a grilled dish that can serve as appetizer or main course. Either way, cool rum beverages, of course, are the ideal accompaniment.

1½ pounds medium-large shrimp, peeled and deveined
⅓ cup coconut-flavored rum
2 tablespoons packed light brown sugar
1½ tablespoons grated fresh ginger with juice
1½ tablespoons fresh lime juice
1½ tablespoons soy sauce
3 cloves garlic, minced
Curried Peanut Dipping Sauce (recipe follows)

In a nonreactive dish, combine the shrimp, rum, sugar, ginger, lime juice, soy sauce, and garlic. Cover and marinate at room temperature, stirring once or twice, for 30 minutes.

Light a charcoal fire and let it burn down or preheat a gas grill to medium-high. Remove the shrimp from the marinade (reserve it) and thread them onto flat metal skewers.

Grill the shrimp, basting them with the reserved marinade and turning them once, until just cooked through while remaining moist, 6 to 7 minutes total.

Slide the shrimp from the skewers and serve hot or warm. Offer the peanut sauce in small bowls for dipping, or transfer it to a squeeze bottle and decoratively drizzle it over the shrimp.

...curried peanut dipping sauce

MAKES ABOUT 1 CUP

This is also good on grilled chicken or vegetables, and makes a fine dressing for a cold noodle salad.

½ cup smooth supermarket peanut butter
½ cup reduced-sodium canned chicken broth
3 tablespoons Thai-style canned coconut milk (not "lite")
2 serrano chiles, stemmed and chopped
2½ tablespoons soy sauce
2 tablespoons fresh lime juice
1½ tablespoons coconut-flavored rum
1 clove garlic, chopped
¾ teaspoon medium-hot but very flavorful curry powder

In a blender or small food processor, combine all the ingredients and process until smooth. Let stand at room temperature for 1 hour to develop the flavors.

rum-jerked chicken wings

Fiery hot and smoky, grilled chicken, pork, and other meats make up the Jamaican national street dish known as "jerk." Jerk is the marinade, packed with various big Caribbean flavors, not the least of which are rum, allspice, and the ultra-hot chiles known as Scotch bonnets. (These chiles are extremely hot, so handle them with care, and use gloves if possible.) More readily available habanero chiles are close cousins, and add their unique and fruity heat to these addictively spicy chicken wing drumettes.

¾ cup chopped yellow onion

⅓ cup chopped scallion

2 Scotch bonnet or habanero chiles, to taste, stemmed and chopped

3 tablespoons dark rum

2½ tablespoons grated fresh ginger with juice

2½ tablespoons soy sauce

2 tablespoons packed dark brown sugar

2 tablespoons fresh lime juice

2 tablespoons olive oil

1 tablespoon Pickapeppa Sauce

¾ teaspoon ground allspice

¼ teaspoon dry thyme, crumbled

3 pounds chicken wing drumettes

In a food processor, combine the yellow onion, scallion, chiles, rum, ginger, soy sauce, sugar, lime juice, olive oil, Pickapeppa, allspice, and thyme. Process until fairly smooth.

In a nonreactive dish, combine the onion mixture and the drumettes and marinate at room temperature for 1 hour.

Light a charcoal fire and let it burn down or preheat a gas grill (medium-low). Lay the drumettes on the rack, reserving the marinade. Grill the drumettes, turning and basting them often, until they are tender and well browned and the marinade is used up, 25 to 30 minutes. Serve hot or warm.

maui

baby back ribs with...

From Havana to Honolulu, rum follows the equator, a tropical product at heart. Which explains this somewhat cross-cultural recipe. Nuevo Latino chefs in Florida have been turning out guava-glazed ribs for years, using guava paste (you'll find it in Latino groceries and some supermarkets) and rum as the major ingredients. To me, though, it always seems Hawaiian, and so that's the approach my rib party takes.

> **2 sides baby back spareribs, about 2 pounds each**
> **Salt**
> **Freshly ground black pepper**
> **Guava Glaze (recipe follows)**

Position a rack in the middle of the oven and preheat to 400°F.

Season the ribs with salt and pepper, then wrap tightly in separate foil packets. Set the packets on a baking sheet and bake until the ribs are very tender, about 1 hour. Let the ribs cool in the foil. Remove the ribs from the foil, cut them into three- or four-rib sections, and transfer them to the baking sheet (line the sheet with foil for easier cleanup). The ribs can be prepared to this point several hours in advance.

Position a rack in the upper third of the oven and preheat to 400°F. Brush the ribs on all sides with about one third of the glaze and bake for 10 minutes. Brush twice more with the remaining glaze at 10-minute intervals, then continue to bake until the glaze is just beginning to brown, another 10 minutes or so. Serve the ribs hot or warm.

...guava glaze

MAKES ABOUT 3 CUPS

Despite the zesty ingredients, the delicate tropical flavor of the guava remains delightfully evident. This is also good on shrimp, chicken, or other cuts of pork.

1½ cups guava paste
½ cup dark rum
⅓ cup sherry vinegar
¼ cup guava nectar
½ cup Dijon mustard
2 tablespoons packed light brown sugar
2 tablespoons soy sauce
2 tablespoons ketchup
2 tablespoons fresh lime juice
1 tablespoon Worcestershire sauce
1 tablespoon habanero hot sauce
1 teaspoon ground ginger
½ teaspoon onion powder

In a heavy, nonreactive saucepan over low heat, combine all the ingredients. Cook, mashing to dissolve the guava paste, until smooth. Simmer 5 minutes more. Cool to room temperature before using.

The glaze will keep in the refrigerator for 1 week or can be frozen for up to 1 month.

garlicky crab fettuccine
in rum cream sauce

MAKES 4 TO 6 SERVINGS

The natural sweetness of the rum enhances the briny sweetness of the crabmeat. This pasta can be served as either starter or main course, and can use either East Coast (blue) or West Coast (Dungeness) crab.

12 ounces dried imported semolina linguine pasta
Salt
5 tablespoons unsalted butter
¾ cup finely diced sweet red pepper
3 cloves garlic, minced
⅛ teaspoon crushed red pepper
⅓ cup gold rum
1¼ cups heavy whipping cream
1 pound fresh jumbo lump crabmeat, picked over
½ cup thawed and drained tiny frozen peas
¼ cup finely chopped flat-leaf parsley
Freshly grated Parmigiano-Reggiano cheese, for serving
Freshly grated black pepper, for serving

Bring a large pot of water to a boil. Add the linguine, salt the water well, and cook according to package directions until almost tender, about 7 minutes.

Meanwhile, in a large skillet over medium heat, melt the butter. Add the sweet pepper, cover, and cook for 5 minutes. Add the garlic and crushed pepper and cook for 2 minutes. Raise the heat to high, add the rum and cream, and simmer until slightly reduced, about 2 minutes.

Drain the pasta well. Add it to the skillet and cook, tossing and stirring the pasta in the sauce, until it has absorbed half of it, about 2 minutes. Add the crab and peas and continue to cook, tossing and stirring, until the crab and peas are heated through, and the pasta has absorbed most of the sauce and is tender, another 2 minutes or so.

Stir in the parsley, divide the pasta among heated bowls, and serve immediately, passing the cheese and a pepper mill at the table.

For years, rum played a part in upholding the slave trade. Captive Africans were paid for with goods from England, shipped to the Caribbean to work producing molasses, which was turned into rum and then sent to England, to be traded for goods, and so on. A similar triangle existed between Africa, the Caribbean, and New England.

pork *mojo*
roast

with molasses-rum baste and pan vegetables

MAKES 6 SERVINGS

Mojo is an all-purpose lime-juice–based Cuban marinade. Here it adds initial flavor to the roast, which is then mopped during cooking with the remaining *mojo*, plus rum and molasses. The slightly sweet, slightly tart, very garlicky glaze is a nice contrast to the pork and its pan-browned vegetables.

½ cup fresh lime juice

6 tablespoons olive oil

3 cloves garlic, finely chopped

2 teaspoons ground cumin

1 boneless center-cut pork loin roast, about 3 pounds

Salt

Freshly ground black pepper

⅔ cup dark rum

½ cup unsulphured molasses

2 large sweet potatoes, about 2 pounds total,
     peeled and cut into chunks

1 medium-large unpeeled yellow onion, cut into 6 wedges

In a shallow nonreactive dish, combine the lime juice, 4 tablespoons of the oil, the garlic, and cumin. Add the pork, cover, and marinate at room temperature, turning occasionally, for 1 hour.

Position a rack in the middle of the oven and preheat to 350°F.

Transfer the roast to a rack set in a shallow roasting pan (reserve the marinade). Season with salt and pepper. Set the pan in the oven and roast for 30 minutes. Meanwhile, mix the rum and molasses into the reserved *mojo*. In a large bowl, toss the sweet potatoes and onion with the remaining 2 tablespoons olive oil.

Add the vegetables to the pan around the roast. Baste the roast with about one quarter of the *mojo*. Return the pan to the oven, reduce the temperature to 325°F, and continue to roast, basting the pork every 15 minutes with some of the remaining *mojo*. The roast is done when the *mojo* is used up and the meat is nicely glazed, another hour or so. An instant-read thermometer inserted into the center will register 165°F. Transfer the roast to a cutting board and tent with foil.

Return the pan to the oven and continue to roast the vegetables, stirring them often, until they are tender and well glazed with the pan drippings, about 25 minutes.

Carve the roast into thin slices and serve, accompanied by the vegetables.

golden mango-rum chutney

MAKES 4 PINTS

Here's a rum-spiked chutney that retains much of the dazzling gold of the mangoes which are its main ingredient. Because the yield is relatively small, you may prefer to simply refrigerate the jars after they are sealed and omit the water-bath processing. Give a couple as gifts, throw a big curry party, open one with the Thanksgiving turkey or the Easter ham, and they will be gone and it will be time to put up another batch.

8 large mangoes, about 6 pounds total, flesh removed
    from the peels and pits and diced, about 8 cups total
2 cups cider vinegar
2 cups sugar
1 medium-large yellow onion, peeled and chopped
2 sweet red peppers, stemmed, cored, and diced
1½ cups dark raisins
½ cup dark rum
¼ cup grated fresh ginger with juice
¼ cup fresh lime juice
5 cloves garlic
1 tablespoon yellow mustard seed
1½ teaspoons salt
1 teaspoon crushed red pepper
Two 4-inch cinnamon sticks

In a large, heavy nonreactive pot, combine all the ingredients. Set over medium heat and bring to a brisk simmer. Cook, uncovered, skimming any scum that forms on the surface and stirring occasionally, until thick, about 35 minutes. Discard the cinnamon sticks.

Spoon the hot chutney into hot sterilized jars, leaving ½-inch headspace. With a dampened towel, wipe the jar rims clean. Seal with new lids and metal rings. Process the jars in a boiling water bath for 10 minutes. Remove the jars from the bath, cool, and check that the lids have sealed. Refrigerate any jars that do not seal. Let the chutney mellow for 1 month before using.

Paul Revere is said to have been somewhat ambivalent about his midnight ride until a couple of tots of rum fired up his enthusiasm.

french
toast ^ brûlée

The crunchy sugar crust on this rum-soaked French toast makes a fine contrast with the rich, custardy interior. The general idea comes from someone, somewhere, though I've forgotten the details; the recipe is my own. Despite the various sugars, this is not too sweet, so you'll probably want to top it with maple syrup, citrus honey, or some kind of tropical fruit jam—guava or pineapple, for example.

5 large eggs

1¼ cups half-and-half

3 tablespoons dark rum

3 tablespoons granulated sugar

1 tablespoon curaçao or other orange liqueur

1½ teaspoons Vanilla Rum (page 105) or vanilla extract

Big pinch of freshly grated nutmeg

Four 1¼-inch-thick slices from a large loaf of firm white bread

2 tablespoons unsalted butter

8 teaspoons turbinado sugar (see page 25)

Confectioners' sugar, for serving

Syrup or preserves, for serving

In a bowl, thoroughly whisk the eggs. Whisk in the half-and-half, rum, granulated sugar, curaçao, Vanilla Rum, and nutmeg. In a shallow dish just large enough to hold the bread slices in a single layer, pour the egg mixture over the bread. Let stand, carefully turning occasionally, until the bread slices are soaked to their centers with the egg mixture (about 10 minutes, but the time will vary with the texture and freshness of the bread).

On a nonstick electric griddle preheated to 325°F, or in a large, nonstick skillet set over medium-low heat, melt the butter. When it foams, evenly sprinkle the top sides of each bread slice with a teaspoon of the turbinado sugar. With a large spatula, carefully transfer the bread slices, sugar side down, to the hot griddle. Cook until golden and crisp, 4 to 5 minutes. Sprinkle the upper sides of the bread slices evenly with the remaining turbinado sugar, turn and cook until golden and crisp, another 3 to 4 minutes.

Transfer to plates, dust with confectioners' sugar and serve immediately, passing assorted toppings at the table.

Island Spice Flan with
Mango-Strawberry Compote

rum

desserts

fl island spice
an
with ...

Allspice is the fragrant heart of lively Jamaica, which led me to use it in these tender, caramel flans. Never good at leaving well enough alone, I've also added a compote of rum-marinated fruit, which lends both color and even more flavor to these sweet comforts.

1⅓ cups plus ½ cup sugar
½ cup water
3 large eggs
5 large egg yolks
½ teaspoon ground allspice
2 cups heavy whipping cream
1½ cups milk
1 tablespoon Vanilla Rum (page 105) or vanilla extract
¼ teaspoon salt
Mango-Strawberry Compote (recipe follows)

Position a rack in the middle of the oven and preheat to 325°F. Set eight ⅔-cup ramekins or custard cups on the work surface.

In a medium, heavy saucepan, stir together the 1⅓ cups sugar and the water. Stir over medium heat until the sugar dissolves. Raise the heat and boil the sugar mixture without stirring (swirl the pan gently to promote even browning), until the syrup turns a rich amber color, about 8 minutes. Working carefully, divide the hot syrup among the ramekins, using it all. Carefully pick up each ramekin and tilt it to coat the sides with caramel syrup.

In a large bowl, whisk together the eggs, yolks, remaining ½ cup sugar, allspice. In a saucepan over medium heat, combine the cream and milk and bring to a simmer. Gradually whisk this hot mixture into the egg mixture. Stir in the Vanilla Rum and salt. Divide the cream mixture among the prepared ramekins.

Set the ramekins in a shallow roasting pan and add very hot tap water to come halfway up their sides. Set the roasting pan in the oven and bake until the flans are just set, about 45 minutes. Remove from the roasting pan, cool to room temperature, cover, and chill, preferably overnight.

To serve, run the blade of a knife around the edge of each flan. Invert each ramekin above a plate and use the knife blade to break the vacuum. The flans and their caramel sauce will drop onto the plates. Spoon the compote over and around the flans and serve immediately.

. . . mango-strawberry compote

MAKES ABOUT 2 CUPS

1 large mango
1 cup coarsely chopped fresh strawberries
2 tablespoons dark rum
1 tablespoon fresh lime juice
2 teaspoons sugar

Cut the mango flesh away from the pit. Score the flesh into ½-inch cubes and cut them away from the peel. In a bowl combine the mango and the remaining ingredients and let stand at room temperature, stirring once or twice, for 30 minutes before using.

See photograph on page 96.

blue mountain
mocha
coconut
sundaes

MAKES 4 SERVINGS

The heart and soul of these fabulous sundaes is the mocha sauce that follows. Not the kind of fudge sauce that hardens when it hits ice cream, it's thinner, which means it can be used straight from the fridge. And toasted coconut keeps well—all very handy for spontaneous types like me. The sundaes are a great company dessert, but they're also great in bed, while watching Letterman.

⅔ cup sweetened flaked coconut
About ½ pint premium vanilla ice cream, softened
About ½ pint premium coffee ice cream, softened
1⅓ cups Blue Mountain Mocha Sauce (recipe follows)

Position a rack in the middle of the oven and preheat to 375°F. Spread the coconut in a thin, even layer in a cake or pie tin and toast, stirring often, until lightly and evenly browned, 8 to 10 minutes. Cool.

Place one scoop of each flavor ice cream in each of four bowls. Spoon the sauce over the ice cream, dividing it evenly. Sprinkle generously with toasted coconut and serve immediately.

blue mountain mocha sauce

MAKES ABOUT 2⅓ CUPS

If you can locate the terrific but rare coffee beans called Blue Mountain (I somehow think most of Jamaica's output goes into the production of Tia Maria liqueur), by all means use them to brew the coffee base for your mocha sauce. No Blue Mountain? Don't despair—any good-quality dark roast coffee will make great sauce.

12 ounces semisweet chocolate chips
1¼ cups freshly brewed strong dark roast coffee
¼ cup dark rum
Pinch of salt
3 tablespoons Tia Maria
½ teaspoon Vanilla Rum (page 105) or vanilla extract

In a small, heavy saucepan over low heat, combine the chocolate chips, coffee, rum, and salt. Cook, stirring often, until the chocolate has melted. Raise the heat, bring to a simmer, and cook gently, stirring often, for 2 minutes.

Strain the sauce into a storage container and cool to room temperature. Stir in the Tia Maria and vanilla rum. Cover and refrigerate. The sauce will keep for up to 1 month (but rarely lasts that long). Use cold or at room temperature.

cheesecake
with orange-rum-raisin
glaze

MAKES 8 SERVINGS

The rum-soaked raisins are on top of, not baked into, this light, rich, and creamy cheesecake, letting rum-and raisin-lovers enjoy them loud and clear. Two colors of raisins make for increased eye appeal but are not really necessary flavor-wise. Dried sweet cherries can replace some or all of the raisins.

CRUST
1 cup finely and evenly crushed graham cracker crumbs
½ stick unsalted butter, melted and cooled slightly
¼ cup sugar

CAKE
1½ pounds cream cheese, at room temperature
1⅓ cups sugar
4 large eggs
2 tablespoons fresh lemon juice
1 tablespoon Vanilla Rum (page 105) or vanilla extract
Pinch of salt

ORANGE-RUM-RAISIN GLAZE
⅔ cup fresh orange juice
½ cup plus 1 tablespoon dark rum
⅓ cup dark raisins
⅓ cup golden raisins
1 tablespoon cornstarch

For the crust, in a bowl, mix together the crumbs, butter, and sugar until well moistened. Pat firmly into the bottom of a 9-inch springform pan. Refrigerate for 30 minutes.

Position a rack in the middle of the oven and preheat to 350°F.

For the filling, in a food processor, combine the cream cheese, sugar, eggs, lemon juice, Vanilla Rum, and salt. Process, stopping several times to scrape down the work bowl, until smooth. Pour into the prepared pan, set the pan in the oven, and bake until the cake has risen and is evenly but not firmly set from edge to center, about 50 minutes. Transfer to a rack, run a knife around the edge of the cake to release it from the pan, and let cool to room temperature.

For the glaze, in a medium, nonreactive pan, combine the orange juice, ½ cup of the rum, and the dark and golden raisins. Let sit at room temperature for 1 hour. In a small bowl, whisk the remaining tablespoon rum into the cornstarch.

Set the pan over medium heat and bring to a simmer. Whisk in the cornstarch mixture and cook until thick, about 30 seconds. Cool slightly; use while lukewarm.

Spread the glaze over the top of the cake to the sides of the springform pan. Cover and refrigerate overnight. Return to room temperature before releasing the sides of the pan. Cut into wedges to serve.

vanilla
rum

MAKES ABOUT 1 CUP

I made my own ultra-potent vanilla extract (put up in antique glass apothecary jars, for holiday giving) for years, but with vodka. Then my friend and frequent collaborator Michael McLaughlin suggested I try rum instead. Because of their mutual tropical origins and because good wood-aged rum often has flavor notes of vanilla, the two are natural partners, and now I'm a convert. As the level of vanilla in the bottle drops, you can add more rum, up to another half cup or so, before starting over.

5 whole vanilla beans
1 cup best-quality gold rum

Split the vanilla beans lengthwise, then halve them crosswise. In a glass jar (decorative, if desired) combine the vanilla bean pieces and the rum. Cover and let stand at room temperature, shaking the bottle occasionally, for 2 weeks. Stored in a cool, dark place, the vanilla rum will last for 1 year. Use it as you would any good vanilla extract.

ginger-rum balls

When I was a child, rum balls were always around at holiday time, and I was always allowed to eat just one. They seemed exotic and grown-up and tasted awful to me then, too boozy for a kid, although now, of course, I love them and wouldn't let a Christmas go by without turning out a big batch. (Naturally, my own son, who loves even dry-cured Moroccan olives, thinks rum balls are awful. His day will come.)

About 9 ounces good-quality purchased gingersnaps
1 cup pecans
1 cup confectioners' sugar, plus confectioners' sugar on a plate
    for dusting the finished balls
¼ cup My Spiced Rum (page 63) or commercially
        prepared spiced rum
3 tablespoons honey

In a food processor, finely grind the gingersnaps. You should have 2 cups. Transfer them to a bowl. In the processor, grind the pecans, leaving a bit of texture. Transfer the pecans to the bowl with the gingersnap crumbs. Add the 1 cup confectioners' sugar, the rum, and the honey and mix thoroughly (use your hands). Cover and let stand at room temperature for about 15 minutes, to firm the texture. Form the mixture into 1-inch balls. Roll the balls in the confectioners' sugar on the plate. Transfer to an airtight storage container and hold at room temperature. The balls will keep for at least 10 days. Roll the balls in more confectioners' sugar, if desired, just before serving.

pineapple and bananas foster

MAKES 4 SERVINGS

This is the great New Orleans treat, created (for breakfast!) at Brennan's Restaurant in the early 1950s. The original recipe is here transformed just slightly by the inclusion of fresh pineapple, an attractive tropical touch. I like it as a brunch dessert and make it at the stove, thus skipping the showy (and risky) tableside flaming that waiters working for tips must engage in.

4 tablespoons (½ stick) unsalted butter
1 cup packed light brown sugar
¼ cup crème de banane
½ teaspoon ground cinnamon
½ medium pineapple, peeled, cored, and cut into
   1-inch chunks
2 medium, ripe but firm bananas, peeled and cut into
   1-inch chunks
¼ cup white or gold rum
1 tablespoon fresh lemon juice
Premium vanilla ice cream, softened slightly

In a large skillet over low heat, melt together the butter, sugar, crème de banane, and cinnamon. Add the pineapple and simmer, stirring occasionally, for 2 minutes. Add the bananas, rum, and lemon juice and simmer, stirring gently, for 3 minutes.

Place one or two scoops of ice cream on each of four dessert plates or shallow bowls. Spoon the fruit and sauce over and around the ice cream, using it all. Serve immediately.